YOUR WEALTH IS YOUR MINDSET: Achieving Financial Independence by Harnessing the Influence of Your Mindset.

YOUR WEALTH IS YOUR MINDSET

Achieving Financial Independence by Harnessing the Influence of Your Mindset.

By

Ruben M. McDonald

YOUR WEALTH IS YOUR MINDSET: Achieving Financial Independence by Harnessing the Influence of Your Mindset.

Copyright © by Ruben M. McDonald|2024. All rights reserved.

The publisher's content must be obtained prior to this material being copied or reproduced in any way. As a result, the information inside cannot be transferred, stored electronically, or preserved in a database.

No portion of the document may be reproduced, scanned, faxed, or stored without permission from the *publisher or author.*

YOUR WEALTH IS YOUR MINDSET: Achieving Financial Independence by Harnessing the Influence of Your Mindset.

TABLE OF CONTENTS
INTRODUCTION 5
CHAPTER 1 10
   CHANGING YOUR PERSPECTIVE TO ATTRACT WEALTH..10
CHAPTER 2 19
   CREATING WEALTH BY ADOPTING A GROWTH MINDSET AND REWRITING YOUR FINANCIAL STORY 19
CHAPTER 3 35
   ACCEPTING KNOWLEDGE AND DEVELOPMENT IN THE CREATION OF WEALTH 35
CHAPTER 4 43
   USING STRATEGIC INVESTMENTS TO BUILD WEALTH 43
CHAPTER 5 54

MANAGING YOUR MONEY AND DEVELOPING A POSITIVE ATTITUDE 54

CHAPTER 6 66

CHAPTER 7 78

CHAPTER 8 91

RESOURCES FOR CONTINUOUS GROWTH AND MINDSET COACHING 91

Resources For Ongoing Development 98

The Foundation of Wealth is Mindset 102

Create Wealth-Creating a Mentality 110

CONCLUSION 114

INTRODUCTION

In this all-inclusive manual, we'll delve into the ways in which your thinking determines your financial success or failure and how to develop a wealth mindset to achieve these goals and more.

A person's mentality is their set of core ideas, values, and ways of thinking that influence their perspective and behavior in relation to the external environment. A person's frame of mind is the single most important factor in influencing their behavior, choices, and, eventually, their financial success and wealth generation.

In this introductory piece, we will explore the core ideas of mindset and how they relate to the building of wealth. In order to break free from self-limiting ideas, reach one's financial objectives, and build an abundant life, we will also go over the significance of developing a positive money attitude. Firstly, it's crucial to acknowledge that our thinking effects every part of our financial path. The way we think influences our actions and behaviors when it comes to money, from our views about success and money to our attitudes towards taking risks and wealth-building tactics.

One of the important parts of a prosperity mindset is having a positive and empowered relationship with money. This requires changing one's perspective from one of scarcity to one of plenty, which is defined by a belief in limitless possibilities, optimism, and a lack of fear.

When you establish an abundant mindset, you open yourself up to opportunities, possibilities, and innovative solutions for earning wealth and reaching financial freedom. Instead of viewing money as a limited resource, you now view it as a means to an end—the ability to build something of worth, have an influence, and enjoy life to the fullest.

Moreover, mentality effects our financial habits, actions, and outcomes. A wealth mindset fosters good financial practices such as budgeting, saving, investing, and strategic planning. It helps you to make informed decisions about money, take calculated risks, and seek possibilities for growth and prosperity.

In this course, we will discuss practical tactics, attitude adjustments, and tangible activities for creating a wealth mindset and unleashing financial freedom. We'll delve into the power of visualization, affirmations, mindfulness practices, resilience, and mindset coaching to help your journey towards financial success.

Ultimately, "Your Wealth Is Your Mindset" is a blueprint for improving your relationship with money, turning your perspective towards abundance, and taking proactive steps to build the financial future you desire. By accepting the principles and techniques outlined in this guide, you'll be enabled to harness the power of your mindset to attain enduring riches, happiness, and fulfillment.

CHAPTER 1
CHANGING YOUR PERSPECTIVE TO ATTRACT WEALTH

In today's society, developing the proper mindset is just as important as having the correct opportunities or techniques for reaching financial freedom and plenty. The Wealth Mindset Blueprint is a thorough manual created to assist you in changing your perspective and opening the door to wealth, prosperity, and financial success.

The idea of plenty forms the foundation of the Wealth Mindset Blueprint. This fundamental idea deals with changing one's perspective from one of scarcity to one of abundance. It all comes down to realizing that there is plenty of money and opportunity for everyone to prosper in this world. Adopting an abundance mindset exposes you to fresh perspectives, imaginative fixes, and an attitude that draws prosperity and money.

An additional fundamental component of the Wealth Mindset Blueprint is having a positive outlook on money. This entails figuring out which restrictive thoughts you may have about money are preventing you from moving forward. It's about seeing wealth as a tool for generating value and changing the world, and it involves taking an optimistic and powerful stance toward it.

Setting clear financial objectives is essential to bringing your intended results into line with your mentality. With the aid of the Wealth Mindset Blueprint, you may establish attainable, well-defined financial objectives. Whether your goals are to establish a business, save for retirement, or reach a specific income threshold, having clear goals will help you concentrate your efforts on the things that really count. Another essential component of the Wealth Attitude Blueprint is adopting a growth attitude. This way of thinking involves viewing obstacles and failures as chances for development and education. It all comes down to having faith in your capacity to grow, change, and get past setbacks on the path to financial success. Developing a development mindset involves fostering tenacity, resilience, and a willingness to take calculated risks. One of the most important skills for creating and maintaining wealth is mindful wealth management. This entails making attentive financial decisions and being conscious of your spending patterns, savings tactics, and investment selections. You can steer clear of rash decisions, make wise financial decisions, and maintain focus on your long-term financial objectives by engaging in mindfulness practices.

Examining Techniques for Creating Wealth:

The Wealth Mindset Blueprint examines numerous wealth-building tactics that complement your financial objectives and mentality. Whether you're looking to establish a business, invest in stocks, or buy real estate, the blueprint offers insights into various wealth-building options and how to best exploit them for optimal success. The Wealth Mindset Blueprint also places a strong emphasis on financial literacy and education. This entails learning about wealth-building techniques, investing philosophies, and money management. You can take charge of your financial destiny, make wise decisions, and spot opportunities by arming yourself with financial knowledge.

A giving and generous mindset is another key component of the Wealth Mindset Blueprint. This way of thinking entails adopting a giving attitude, helping others, and realizing the power of abundance that results from giving. Including philanthropy and charitable giving in your wealth-building endeavors not only helps other people but also fulfills you personally. Appreciation and thankfulness exercises are an essential part of the Wealth Mindset Blueprint. Acknowledging and appreciating the richness in your life—whether it be opportunities, supporting relationships, or financial blessings—is the essence of gratitude. You may draw more riches, happiness, and prosperity into your life by practicing thankfulness. Taking Initiative and Responsibility: The Wealth Mindset Blueprint places a strong emphasis on the necessity of acting consistently to achieve your financial objectives. This entails establishing concrete goals, maintaining discipline, and remaining devoted to your mission. Seeking mentors or accountability partners can help you stay accountable to your goals and assist you on your journey.

The Wealth Mindset Blueprint is a transformative path towards financial prosperity and freedom, not merely a manual. You may realize your financial dreams, reach your full potential, and build a prosperous, fulfilling life by adopting the ideas, tactics, and mental changes described in the blueprint.

CHAPTER 2

CREATING WEALTH BY ADOPTING A GROWTH MINDSET AND REWRITING YOUR FINANCIAL STORY

More than simply financial literacy and tactics are needed to achieve financial plenty and build long-term wealth—a fundamental mentality shift is needed. Changing your money story, redefining your financial beliefs, and embracing a growth mindset are the first steps on the path to financial success. This extensive book will cover the mentality changes required for financial abundance as well as the development of a growth attitude for wealth building.

Developing a growth mindset to create wealth is the idea that aptitude and intelligence can be improved with commitment and effort. A growth mentality is necessary for wealth development in order to overcome obstacles, seize opportunities, and never stop learning and developing. To create wealth, it's important to embrace the following fundamentals of a growth mindset: Developing the correct mindset is just as important to wealth building as financial methods and possibilities. A growth mentality is a potent tool that can revolutionize the way you create money and support you in achieving long-term financial success. The main ideas of developing a growth mentality for wealth development will be covered in this tutorial, along with how it might lead to new prospects.

Understanding the Growth mentality: The idea that aptitude and intelligence can be enhanced by commitment, work, and education is known as the growth mentality. Growth-minded people welcome challenges, keep going after obstacles, and view failure as a chance for improvement and education. This kind of thinking is crucial for building wealth because it promotes resilience, constant development, and a willingness to accept measured risks. Fundamentals of Developing a Growth Mindset to Create Wealth:

Accept Challenges: Growth-minded individuals view obstacles as chances for development and education. Rather of running from difficulties or failures, they welcome them as opportunities to grow in understanding, expertise, and understanding. Adopting a challenge-welcoming mindset when it comes to wealth creation enables you to discover new opportunities, innovate, and get beyond roadblocks on your way to financial success.

Gain Knowledge from Feedback: Getting feedback is a great way to develop and get better. People that possess a growth mentality actively seek out input from mentors, peers, and experts in order to acquire new perspectives, pinpoint areas that require development, and hone their tactics. They see criticism as a helpful tool that will help them develop and improve the outcomes of their wealth-building projects.

Persistence and Resilience: All of these qualities are necessary for creating wealth; they also include a readiness to keep going in the face of obstacles and disappointments. Growth-minded people recognize that obstacles are a normal part of the road and that success is not necessarily linear. They maintain their resilience, learn from their mistakes, and maintain their long-term objectives and vision in focus.

Accept Learning and Growth: A growth mindset is based on the ideas of lifelong learning and personal advancement. Curiosity, open-mindedness, and a desire to learn new things are characteristics of those who have this mindset. They take an interest in learning, pursue educational opportunities, and maintain their adaptability in a world that is changing quickly. Embracing learning and growth in the context of wealth building enables you to remain up to date on financial possibilities, investing techniques, and market trends.

Change Your attitude from Fixed to Growth: Changing your attitude from a fixed to a growth mindset is one of the most important changes you can do to create riches. A fixed mindset is typified by the conviction that intelligence and skill are unchangeable fixed attributes. This kind of thinking might impede your capacity to take chances and seize opportunities, limit your potential, and induce self-doubt. To adopt a growth mentality instead than a fixed one:

- Contest limiting assumptions: Determine whatever beliefs are preventing you from taking chances or pursuing opportunities to build wealth, and then confront them.

Accept failure as a teaching tool: See setbacks as chances to develop, learn, and refine your methods.

"- Have faith in your capacity to change and adapt: As you embark on your wealth building journey, have faith in your ability to learn, adapt, and overcome obstacles.

Example Study: Sarah's Path to Creating Wealth by Using a Growth Mindset

As a young businesswoman, Sarah first battled self-doubt and failure-apprehension related to wealth accumulation. Her fixed thinking prevented her from believing she could succeed and take chances. But Sarah changed the way she approached wealth creation with mindset coaching, personal development, and a growth mentality.

Sarah saw obstacles as chances to improve and gain knowledge. She stayed strong in her pursuit of financial success, persevered in the face of obstacles, and asked mentors and peers for advice. Her mentality changed from fixed to growing, and she began to believe that she could learn, progress, and accomplish her objectives of creating riches.

Embracing obstacles, receiving feedback, building resilience, and transitioning from a fixed to a growth mentality are all part of the transforming process of adopting a growth mindset for wealth creation. Through the implementation of these fundamental ideas and mentalities, you can open doors, get beyond challenges, and attain prosperity and long-term financial success.

Modifying Your Financial Narrative and Recasting Money-Related Beliefs:

Childhood experiences, cultural influences, and previous financial hardships are typically the source of our attitudes and views toward money. It is imperative that you reframe your thoughts about money and adjust your money story in order to reach financial plenty. Key techniques for rewriting your financial narrative and redefining your financial ideas are as follows:

Changing Perceptions Regarding Finance

Think about Sarah's experience. She is a young professional whose family was frequently tense and stressed up over money. Sarah absorbed notions of deprivation, scarcity, and the necessity of enduring hardship in order to survive. She thus discovered herself trapped in a vicious circle of monetary instability and constrictive money views.

But in order to attain financial abundance, Sarah understood that she had to rewrite her financial history and recast her money-related attitudes. She began by recognizing her limiting ideas and countering them with empowering thoughts that complemented her financial objectives. She adopted an attitude of abundance rather than scarcity, concentrating on possibilities, chances, and thankfulness for the abundance that was already there in her life.

Sarah adopted a growth mindset in order to create riches, seeing obstacles as chances for development, education, and advancement. She was resolute in the face of obstacles, kept up her efforts, and asked mentors for advice. Sarah changed her perspective and attained financial wealth and independence via self-improvement, ongoing learning, and rewriting her financial story.

It takes a development mentality, a rewritten money story, and a reinterpretation of money-related ideas to transform your thinking for financial abundance. A mindset that promotes wealth development and success can be developed by accepting obstacles, taking constructive criticism to heart, persevering through difficulties, and changing your perspective from one of scarcity to abundance. Finding your limiting beliefs, rewriting your story, and developing a wealth mindset that is in line with opportunities, prosperity, and success are all part of changing your money story. You can discover the way to financial abundance, reach your financial objectives, and design a life of riches, happiness, and fulfillment by engaging in mindset exercises and shifts.

CHAPTER 3
ACCEPTING KNOWLEDGE AND DEVELOPMENT IN THE CREATION OF WEALTH

Our guide's fourth chapter discusses the value of accepting lifelong learning and personal development in the framework of wealth creation. Achieving financial success in today's environment of rapid change requires being knowledgeable, flexible, and open-minded. The methods for accepting learning and development are covered in this chapter, along with how they might improve your path to wealth creation.

The Power of Continuous Learning: Developing a growth mindset and creating wealth are directly related to continuous learning. Maintaining your curiosity, pursuing new information, and developing your abilities and knowledge can help you stay ahead of the curve and take advantage of new possibilities as they arise in the financial world. You may also make better decisions, adjust to changes in the market, and improve your strategy with ongoing learning.

Seeking Educational Possibilities: Finding learning opportunities on your own is crucial if you want to embrace growth and learning. Formal education in the form of classes, seminars, and workshops on entrepreneurship, finance, and investing can fall under this category. In addition, reading books, articles, blogs, and podcasts written by subject-matter experts can all be considered informal learning methods.

3. Investing in Your Education: Making a strategic investment in your education can help you create wealth. In order to

improve your knowledge and abilities in areas related to your financial goals, you may choose to pursue higher degrees, certificates, or specialized training. Investing time, money, and energy in continuing education can pay off in the long run by increasing your chances of financial success.

4. Remaining Flexible and Open-Minded: Encouraging learning and development requires remaining flexible and open-minded. Be open to investigating fresh viewpoints, tactics, and concepts that contradict your preconceived notions and views.

Continue to be open to criticism, look for different perspectives, and be adaptable in your wealth-building strategies.

Mentoring and networking: You can learn and advance in wealth creation more quickly by pursuing mentorship from seasoned professionals and networking with like-minded people. Seek for chances for cooperation and knowledge exchange, surround yourself with supportive people, and gain insight and experience from others who have succeeded financially.

Putting Knowledge into Practice:

It takes more than simply knowledge acquisition to embrace learning and growth; it also requires putting that knowledge into practice. Use everything you've discovered to enhance your wealth-building tactics. Try things out, refine your plan based on criticism and the outcome. Iteratively improve your strategy in light of fresh knowledge and understanding acquired throughout education.

Integrating Lifelong Learning with Wealth Creation

Take the example of John, a prosperous investor who credits his dedication to lifelong learning for a large portion of his achievements. John keeps up with market developments and investment opportunities by reading financial magazines, attending industry conferences, and attending networking events on a monthly basis. He also looks to seasoned investors for mentorship, as they offer insightful advice.

John has been able to recognize new

market trends, take advantage of investment possibilities, and successfully negotiate market swings thanks to his constant learning. A major factor in his wealth development journey has been his willingness to adapt, learn from criticism, and maintain an open mind.

It is emphasized how crucial it is to embrace lifelong learning and personal development in order to create riches. You can attain long-term wealth creation objectives and improve your financial performance by remaining inquisitive, looking for learning opportunities, investing in education, remaining flexible and open-minded, networking, and putting information into practice. Accepting knowledge and development is not merely a way of thinking; it's a calculated move that can help you achieve success and financial prosperity.

CHAPTER 4
USING STRATEGIC INVESTMENTS TO BUILD WEALTH

Our guide's Chapter 4 explores the topic of strategic investments and their critical role in generating wealth. To maximize profits and meet long-term financial objectives, strategic investing entails distributing your resources—financial or otherwise—in a planned and methodical way. This chapter covers a variety of strategic investment options, important guidelines to follow, and methods for increasing wealth via wise financial choices.

Comprehending Strategic Investments: These comprise a diverse array of options and asset types, such as equities, bonds, real estate, venture capital, and alternative investments. Long-term financial objectives, capital preservation, and wealth generation are the three main aims of strategic investment. Strategic investments, as opposed to speculative or short-term ones, are supported by extensive study, long-term planning, and research.

Categorization of Strategic Investments:

Equity: Investing in equity entails buying shares of corporations that are listed on a public exchange, giving ownership rights as well as the chance for dividends and capital growth.

Fixed Income: Compared to stocks, fixed income assets, such bonds and government securities, offer consistent income streams and lower risk.

Real estate investments: These include houses, businesses, and rental properties. They provide chances for portfolio diversification, capital growth, and income production.

Business ventures: While there is a chance for large gains, there is also a bigger risk when investing in startups, small enterprises, or entrepreneurial endeavors.

Alternative Investments: Although they offer diversification and the possibility of larger profits, alternative investments include commodities, hedge funds, private equity, and cryptocurrencies also come with a higher risk and require specialist understanding.

Essential Ideas for Strategic Investments:

Effective risk management is crucial for protecting capital and minimizing potential losses in strategic investment. Risk can be reduced by diversifying investments across sectors, regions, and asset classes.

Due Diligence: Before making an investment, careful study, analysis, and due diligence are essential. Assess the state of the finances, past performance, management group, level of competition, and market trends.

Long-Term Perspective: The emphasis of strategic investment is on attaining financial objectives over a protracted period of time as opposed to short-term benefits. Remain disciplined in your investing technique and refrain from responding to transient market changes.

Asset Allocation: Taking into account investment goals, time horizon, and risk tolerance, strategic asset allocation identifies the best combination of asset classes. To attain diversification and balance the risk-reward profile, carefully allocate resources.

Regular Monitoring and Review:
Keep an eye on your investments to make sure they're in line with your financial objectives, risk tolerance, and shifting market circumstances. To keep the appropriate asset allocation in your portfolio, frequently rebalance it.

Techniques for Increasing Wealth via Wise Investments:
To take advantage of cost averaging and lessen the effect of market volatility on investment returns, consistently invest over time,

irrespective of market swings. This is known as dollar-cost averaging.

Value investing involves identifying assets or securities that are inexpensive but have excellent fundamentals and the ability to grow over time. Invest in reputable businesses with long-term business plans and competitive advantages.

Income Investing: Pay particular attention to investments that yield consistent income streams, like income-producing assets, rental properties, dividend-paying stocks, and bonds.

Investing in growth: Look for assets like growth equities, emerging markets, or cutting-edge industries that have the potential to see substantial capital growth and accumulation.

Tax-efficient investing involves making the most out of tax techniques and utilizing tax-deferred accounts, tax-efficient investments, and tax-loss harvesting to reduce tax obligations and improve after-tax returns.

A Case Study of a Successful Strategic Investment

Think about Emily, a methodical

investor who distributes her funds wisely among a variety of asset classes. Emily takes a long-term view, performs extensive due diligence and research, and keeps a disciplined approach to investing. Depending on her risk tolerance and financial objectives, she balances her portfolio with a combination of fixed income, real estate, stocks, and alternative assets. Emily preserves capital throughout market downturns, builds wealth over time, and consistently generates returns through prudent investments. Her long-term financial success is a result of her careful asset allocation, investing techniques, and risk management. Strategic investments play a critical role in wealth generation, as discussed. You may avoid risk, reach your financial objectives, and make well-informed investment selections by being aware of the many kinds of strategic investments as well as important concepts and techniques. A long-term outlook, thorough planning, research, and risk management are all necessary for strategic investing. You may accumulate wealth, protect cash, and safeguard your financial future by putting strategic investment plans into practice.

CHAPTER 5
MANAGING YOUR MONEY AND DEVELOPING A POSITIVE ATTITUDE

Financial difficulties are a typical aspect of life and can be brought on by a number of things, including unforeseen costs, job loss, downturns in the economy, or bad financial choices. Nevertheless, our capacity to overcome problems and attain success and financial stability is frequently determined by how we approach and manage these difficulties. This tutorial will examine the ways in which developing a strong attitude can assist people in overcoming obstacles related to money, strengthening their resilience, and paving the way for financial well-being.

Comprehending the Influence of Mentality: Mentality is the fundamental convictions, outlooks, and attitudes that mold our feelings, ideas, and actions. The traits of a strong mindset include adaptability, resilience, optimism, and a readiness to grow and learn from setbacks. When it comes to conquering financial obstacles, our response and actions are greatly influenced by our mindset.

The Transition from a State of Scarcity to a State of Abundance:

Changing from a scarcity to an abundant mindset is one of the key mentalities to overcome financial obstacles. The characteristics of a scarcity mindset are shortage, dread, and the idea that there is never enough. Conversely, an abundance mindset stems from the conviction that there are an abundance of resources, opportunities, and solutions accessible. How to change your perspective from one of scarcity to abundance? - Develop thankfulness by concentrating on what you have rather than what you lack. Being grateful helps you maintain an optimistic attitude and draws more prosperity into your life.

Visualize success: Envision yourself accomplishing your objectives, overcoming financial obstacles, and leading an abundant life. Action is motivated and positive thoughts are reinforced through visualization.

Have a development mentality: Accept

obstacles as chances to improve and gain knowledge. Consider obstacles as temporary and use lessons from mistakes to advance and get better. Building a Robust Financial Portfolio: Resilience is the capacity to overcome obstacles, adjust to change, and recover from failures. Having a plan to efficiently navigate financial problems, controlling risks, and constructing a solid foundation are all components of financial resilience. The following are essential components of financial resilience: - Emergency savings: Establish an emergency fund to handle unforeseen costs and financial crises.

Financial planning and budgeting:

Establish a spending plan, keep tabs on outlays, and make plans for future objectives and costs.

Financial strategies, investments, and income streams should all be diversified in order to lower risk and boost resilience.

The right insurance coverage, such as life, health, and property insurance, can help you safeguard your assets and yourself.

Cultivating a good Money Mindset:

Breaking through financial obstacles

and reaching financial success require a good money mindset. It entails embracing positive attitudes and ideas about money, such as the following: - I am capable of managing my finances and making wise financial decisions; - Financial challenges are opportunities for learning and growth; - I can create abundance and prosperity in my life through wise financial choices.

To develop a good outlook on money: Recite affirmations aloud: Use empowering affirmations to reaffirm your views about success and money. Become informed: Develop your financial literacy and understanding to take charge of your finances and make wise decisions.

Surround yourself with uplifting people: Seek resources, mentors, and role models who encourage and assist you in achieving your financial objectives.

Act: Make a plan, establish a budget, and work consistently to reach your goals.

Looking for Resources and Assistance:

Although overcoming financial difficulties can seem overwhelming, you don't have to accomplish it by yourself. To overcome obstacles and develop financial resilience, look for assistance, direction, and resources: Financial counselors: Seek counsel and direction on managing your funds from a financial counselor or planner. Assistance systems: Make connections with family, friends, or support groups that can provide words of wisdom, practical help, and encouragement. Educational resources: To improve your financial knowledge and abilities, make use of books, workshops, and courses on finance.

Overcoming Adversity in Money with a Positive Attitude

Think about Alex's experience, who lost his work during a recession and had to deal with financial difficulties. Instead of giving in to hopelessness and anxiety, Alex developed a resilient attitude and made aggressive moves to go past his obstacles:

Alex adopted an abundant attitude,

keeping a cheerful outlook, believing in his own ability to recover, and concentrating on possibilities.

Developed financial resilience: He looked for alternate sources of income, made a budget, and utilized his emergency funds to pay bills.

Developed a positive money mindset: Alex read up on personal finance, made affirmations, and talked to a financial expert for advice.

Action: He revised his resume, made industry contacts through networking, and persistently looked for new employment options.

By maintaining a positive attitude and taking initiative, Alex was able to overcome his financial obstacles, land a new career, and increase his financial resilience and self-assurance going forward.

Financial difficulties must be overcome with more than simply financial know-how or tactics; proactive thinking, resilience, and strong will are also necessary. People can overcome obstacles, achieve financial stability, and pave the way for financial well-being and success by adopting an abundance attitude rather than a scarcity one, becoming financially resilient, adopting a positive money perspective, getting help, and acting. Financial difficulties can be transformed into chances for development, education, and prosperity if you have the correct perspective.

CHAPTER 6
MASTERING YOUR MINDSET FOR INVESTING AND WEALTH MANAGEMENT

It takes more than just financial know-how and tactics to succeed in investing and wealth management; you also need to have the correct mindset. Gaining the attitudes, convictions, and behaviors necessary for wise investing choices, long-term wealth accumulation, and financial security is known as mindset mastery. The main ideas of wealth management and investment mentality mastery, as well as how they might result in prosperity and financial success, will be covered in this handbook.

Having an Investor Mentality: Having an investor mindset is the first step toward mastering investing mindset. With this kind of thinking, investing is seen as a long-term endeavor, risk is accepted as a necessary component, and core values are prioritized before quick profits. A mindset of an investor should focus on the following essentials:

Patience: Recognizing that investing is a marathon rather than a sprint, as well as having patience with volatility and changes in the market.

Self-control: adhering to a financial strategy, refraining from rash choices, and keeping an eye on the big picture.

Research and analysis: gathering information, examining investment prospects, and drawing deft conclusions from data and fundamentals.

Risk management: This includes adjusting risk tolerance levels, diversifying investment holdings, and controlling risk by allocating assets and rebalancing portfolios.

Getting Rid of Emotional Biases: Emotions frequently impair judgment and cause people to make illogical investment decisions. Mastering a mindset is overcoming emotional prejudices and choosing to make decisions based on reason and analysis as opposed to instinct or greed. Fear of missing out (FOMO) is a common emotional bias in investing that can result in rash judgments and following after fads in the market without doing adequate study or analysis.

Loss aversion: Investors who are

fearful of losing money may be unable to take calculated risks or adhere to long-term investing plans.

Overconfidence: Taking unnecessary risks and making bad decisions might result from overestimating one's skills or the certainty of investment outcomes.

To get above emotional prejudices: Make mindfulness a habit: Recognize how your feelings might affect your decision-making when it comes to investing. Step back and evaluate circumstances with objectivity.

Create a plan: Make an investing

strategy with specific objectives, degrees of risk tolerance, and rules for making decisions. Even when the market fluctuates, stay true to your goal.

Look for a variety of viewpoints: Discuss your concerns and obtain alternative perspectives by speaking with friends, mentors, or financial advisors.

Make use of technology and tools: Make data-driven judgments and lessen emotional biases by utilizing software, data analytics, and investment tools.

Developing Self-Belief and

Adaptability:

In order to grasp the attitude of investing and wealth management, one must possess resilience and confidence. Believing in your skills, expertise, and ability to make decisions is a key component in developing confidence. Resilience is the capacity to overcome obstacles, draw lessons from mistakes, and adjust to shifting market conditions. Important techniques to develop resilience and confidence include:

Ongoing Education: Keep up with changes in the economy, investment tactics, and market trends. Make an investment in your knowledge and abilities to improve your judgment and self-assurance.

Analyze your investment track record, including past successes and failures. Make better decisions in the future by applying what you've learned from the past.

Use affirmations and an optimistic outlook to bolster your resilience, confidence, and investment performance.

Maintain long-term goals in mind: Pay close attention to your long-term financial goals and ambitions. You should stick to your main investing strategy despite brief market changes or setbacks.

Changes in Mentality that Promote Wealth Creation: Developing certain mentalities that promote wealth creation and financial abundance is another aspect of mastering the mind. Among these mental adjustments are: Having an abundance mindset is viewing possibilities, wealth growth, and abundance as superior to scarcity or lack.

Growth mindset: accepting challenges,

picking up from mistakes, and advancing knowledge and abilities constantly.

A financial owner is someone who accepts accountability for their money choices, deeds, and results. eschewing a victim or blaming mindset.

Collaboration mindset: aiming to maximize group possibilities, resources, and expertise via cooperation, partnership, and teamwork.

Examine the example of Maria, an investor who developed a strong mentality and succeeded financially by using resilience and disciplined investing:

Investor mentality: Maria gave up chasing after fads or quick profits in favor of a long-term investor mentality based on fundamentals.

Emotional mastery: She overcome her emotional prejudices, maintained her composure throughout market turbulence, and made logical choices based on investigation and evaluation.

Resilience and confidence: Maria learned from her mistakes, adjusted her tactics in response to shifting market conditions, and gained confidence in her investing choices.

Changes in mindset: She adopted an attitude of plenty, expansion, ownership, and collaboration, all of which aided in the construction of her fortune.

Gaining mastery of one's mindset is essential for managing wealth and investing successfully. Investors can negotiate obstacles, make wise judgments, and accumulate long-term wealth by accepting particular mindset modifications, overcoming emotional biases, developing confidence, and developing resilience. Mastering a mindset is a constant process that calls for practice, self-awareness, and ongoing education. Investors may reach their financial objectives, realize their full potential, and build prosperous, abundant lives with the correct mindset.

CHAPTER 7
PROVIDING A GENERATIONAL WEALTH MINDSET

The resources, assets, and financial legacy that are passed down from one generation to the next are referred to as generational wealth. In order to generate and maintain generational wealth, one must foster a wealth mindset, which entails developing attitudes, behaviors, and beliefs that promote long-term financial success and prosperity. We'll go over the fundamentals of cultivating a wealth mindset for generational wealth in this book, along with how it can help present and future generations.

Comprehending Generational Wealth: This concept extends beyond monetary holdings; it also includes opportunities, values, knowledge, and abilities that are passed down via families. It offers a base on which succeeding generations can construct, generate possibilities, and realize their own potential. Strategic financial planning, investments, entrepreneurship, and a strong emphasis on education and personal growth are frequently used to create generational wealth.

Developing a Wealth Mindset:
Beliefs, attitudes, and actions that promote success, financial abundance, and long-term prosperity are the hallmarks of a wealth mindset. Developing a wealth mindset entails the following: - Abundance attitude: Holding the view that opportunities, wealth creation potential, and abundance outweigh scarcity or lack. A growth mentality involves accepting obstacles, growing from setbacks, and

always enhancing one's abilities. Having an ownership mindset is accepting accountability for one's financial choices, deeds, and results. avoiding taking the blame for others or adopting a victim mindset.

Legacy mindset: Planning forward and taking into account how financial actions may affect coming generations. putting the transfer of assets between generations and wealth preservation first.

Values and Principles of Generational Wealth: Developing a wealth mindset for future generations of wealth entails imparting values and principles that encourage resource management and financial success. Important ideals and guidelines consist of:

Financial literacy: Teaching family members from a young age about investing, budgeting, money management, and financial planning. Entrepreneurship: Fostering a sense of inventiveness, business savvy, and entrepreneurial spirit inside the family. assisting family-run companies and projects.

Long-term vision: Considering the

effects of financial actions on future generations and looking beyond the here and now. preparing for a number of generations.

Philanthropy: Integrating social responsibility, community influence, and charitable giving into wealth management strategies and family values.

Collaboration: Encouraging harmony, cooperation, and communication within the family to match values, financial objectives, and approaches between generations.

Techniques for Developing a Wealth-

Sentiment:

Sharing of information and education: Family members should be given information, workshops, and seminars on financial planning, investments, and wealth management.

Set an example for others to follow: Set an example for the next generation by practicing responsible financial conduct, thoughtful decision-making, and long-term planning.

Make a financial plan for the family: Create a thorough wealth plan that details your objectives, principles, investment approach, estate planning, and generational wealth transfer plans. Encourage candid dialogue: Encourage family members to communicate honestly, openly, and cooperatively about money-related issues, objectives, worries, and dreams.

Consult a professional: Obtain advice from estate planners, financial advisors, and legal specialists to develop specialized plans for asset protection, wealth preservation, and intergenerational transfer.

Legacy Building and Wealth Preservation: To guarantee that wealth is passed down through the generations, cultivating a wealth mindset also entails using legacy building and wealth preservation techniques. Important tactics consist of:

Estate planning: To ensure a seamless transfer of assets and reduce tax implications, create a thorough estate plan that includes wills, trusts, and succession plans.

Asset allocation: To lower risk and protect money over time, diversify your investments across industries, locations, and asset classes.

Risk management: To preserve wealth against unanticipated catastrophes, put risk management techniques into practice, such as insurance coverage, asset protection, and contingency planning.

Financial stewardship: To preserve and increase family wealth, instill in family members the values of accountable, responsible, and cautious financial management.

Continuity planning: To manage family wealth and enterprises over generations, develop a continuity plan that specifies roles, duties, governance structures, and succession plans.

Case Study: The Journey to Wealth by

the Smith Family

The Smith family is a multigenerational family that has developed generational wealth over several decades by effectively cultivating a wealth mindset. Along the way, they have: Financial education and knowledge exchange were given top priority by the Smith family, who supplied tools, conferences, and seminars to teach family members about investments and wealth management.

Principles and values: The Smith family aligned financial decisions with family values and objectives by incorporating concepts of entrepreneurship, creativity, generosity, and long-term vision into their wealth management processes.

Legacy building: To guarantee the preservation and transfer of wealth between generations, the Smith family developed an extensive wealth strategy that included asset allocation, risk management, estate planning, and continuity planning.

Cooperation and communication: By promoting active engagement, shared decision-making, and alignment of financial objectives, the Smith family promoted open communication, cooperation, and togetherness among family members.

Developing a wealth mindset for generational wealth is a complex process that calls for intergenerational cooperation, education, ideals, and tactics. Generational wealth can be safeguarded and transmitted to subsequent generations through the adoption of an abundance mindset, the adoption of fundamental values and principles, the application of strategic wealth management techniques, and the promotion of open communication and cooperation within the family members. The secret to leaving a lasting financial legacy and guaranteeing success for future generations is mastering your mindset.

CHAPTER 8
RESOURCES FOR CONTINUOUS GROWTH AND MINDSET COACHING

Because it concentrates on developing attitudes, behaviors, and beliefs that promote success, growth, and resilience, mindset coaching is an effective tool for both professional and personal development. We'll go over the significance of mindset coaching, its guiding principles, and the tools accessible for ongoing development and progress in this guide.

Comprehending Mindset Coaching: Mindset coaching is a type of coaching that concentrates on assisting people in overcoming limiting beliefs, cultivating a positive outlook, and accomplishing their objectives. It entails methods, plans, and activities designed to change thought habits, develop self-awareness, and enable people to realize their greatest potential. Numerous facets of mindset are addressed by mindset coaching, such as:

Growth mindset: accepting of obstacles, taking lessons from setbacks, and having faith in one's capacity to advance and prosper.

A resilient mindset entails overcoming obstacles, adjusting to change, and keeping an optimistic view in the face of hardship.

An abundant mindset is the conviction that there is more opportunity, abundance, and potential for success than there is lack or scarcity.

Empowerment mindset: Taking responsibility for one's feelings, ideas, and behavior and bringing about constructive change in one's life.

Essential Ideas in Mindset Coaching

Self-awareness: The basis of mindset coaching is the development of self-awareness. It entails realizing how one's attitudes, convictions, feelings, and actions affect objectives and results.

Growth mentality: Fostering a growth mindset entails supporting people in accepting criticism, persevering in the face of setbacks, and viewing difficulties as chances for learning and development.

Goal-setting: A key component of mindset coaching is the establishment of precise, attainable goals. Objectives offer guidance, inspiration, and a plan for ongoing development.

Positive reinforcement: Giving constructive criticism, encouragement, and support helps to reinforce desired behavioral changes and mindset adjustments, which boost self-esteem and motivation.

Accountability: Accountability, discipline, and responsibility are fostered when people are held responsible for their deeds, promises, and advancement toward objectives.

Advantages of Coaching for Mindset: Numerous advantages of mindset coaching exist for both professional and personal development, such as: Gained more resilience and the capacity to overcome obstacles Enhanced dedication, desire, and motivation to achieve goals Increased clarity, focus, and direction in life and profession; improved leadership and interpersonal skills; improved decision-making and problem-solving abilities; decreased stress and anxiety; and altered negative thought patterns

Exercises & Techniques For Mindset Coaching:

Reframing beliefs: Recognize and confront limiting beliefs, transform negative ideas into empowering statements, and develop beliefs that enable development and achievement.

Visualization: Make a mental blueprint for desired outcomes and envision yourself accomplishing goals by using visualization techniques.

Mindfulness: To develop self-awareness, lower stress levels, and sharpen attention, engage in mindfulness techniques including meditation, deep breathing, and attentive awareness.

Goal-setting: Establish action plans, make SMART goals (Specific, Measurable, Achievable, Relevant, Time-bound), and monitor your progress on a regular basis.

Practice gratitude: Develop a mindset of thankfulness by thanking God every day for all of your benefits, successes, and enjoyable times.

Resources For Ongoing Development

Books: Examine books by writers like

Tony Robbins ("Awaken the Giant Within"), Brendon Burchard ("High Performance Habits"), and Carol Dweck ("Mindset: The New Psychology of Success") on mentality, personal growth, and achievement. Online courses: Join online programs and courses offered by sites like Coursera, Udemy, and LinkedIn Learning that are centered on mindset coaching, personal development, leadership, and emotional intelligence.

Workshops and seminars: Participate in mindset coaching, resilience, goal-setting, and personal empowerment workshops, seminars, and conferences led by knowledgeable coaches and trainers.

Mentoring initiatives: Consult with a trained coach or mindset coach with expertise in goal-achieving, personal change, and mindset coaching. Get individualized help, direction, and responsibility to realize your greatest potential.

Podcasts and videos: Watch and listen to podcasts where thought leaders, motivational speakers, and mindset trainers share ideas, tactics, and inspiration for ongoing personal improvement.

One of the most effective tools for achievement, personal growth, and ongoing progress is mindset coaching. People can realize their full potential, accomplish their goals, and have satisfying lives by embracing growth mindset, positive beliefs, mindset coaching activities, and tools for ongoing learning and development. With the help of mindset coaching, people may overcome obstacles, develop resilience, and bring about positive change in all facets of their lives, which increases their success, happiness, and contentment.

The path to financial freedom by the application of discipline and mentality demands commitment, self-awareness, and ongoing development. In investigating the idea behind the title "Your wealth is your mindset," we have looked at the core ideas and how they can change a person's financial situation. It's important to consider the most important lessons learned and realizations that come from realizing the significant influence of discipline and mindset on reaching financial freedom as we wrap up our conversation.

The Foundation of Wealth is Mindset

"Your wealth is your mindset" is based on the understanding that our perspectives, attitudes, and beliefs influence how we behave financially. A growth-oriented, optimistic mindset is the cornerstone of financial success. We may change our perspective from one of scarcity and constraint to one of abundance and opportunity by embracing an abundance mindset. This change in perspective enables us to recognize opportunities where others perceive barriers, grasp chances for personal development, and develop resilience in the face of difficulty. Furthermore, our mentality affects how we view money, prosperity, and success. Our ideas and attitudes about money can be reframed to fit wealth-building principles by addressing limiting beliefs like self-doubt, fear of failure, or scarcity. For instance, seeing money as a tool for impact and value creation rather than a cause of worry or anxiety might enable us to explore growth opportunities and make prudent financial decisions.

The Power of Discipline in Financial Success

Financial freedom can only be attained via disciplined thinking combined with discipline. Discipline includes routines, attitudes, and acts that support our beliefs and financial objectives. It entails exercising self-control when handling money, making deliberate decisions, and giving long-term objectives precedence over instant gratification.

A number of financial management tasks, such as budgeting, saving, investing, and debt management, require discipline. We build the foundation for financial stability and growth by forming responsible financial practices including making a budget, keeping track of spending, saving consistently, and abstaining from impulsive purchases. Investing methods are another area where discipline is required. We must stick to our objectives, diversify our portfolios, and avoid making rash decisions when the market is fluctuating.

Furthermore, discipline helps us pursue our financial goals with regularity and tenacity. It supports us in maintaining our resilience, motivation, and focus in the face of difficulties or failures. We create a strong foundation for long-term financial success and stability by fostering discipline in our financial routines and decision-making processes.

Constant Learning and Development: Achieving financial freedom requires constant learning, development, and adaptation. It necessitates a dedication to personal development, knowledge of finances, and keeping up with changing possibilities and trends in the economy. We may increase our knowledge, abilities, and skills in handling money wisely and coming to wise financial decisions by continuing to learn. Adopting a growth mentality also pushes us to see challenges, setbacks, and failures as chances for improvement. Rather than letting obstacles depress us, we use them as teaching opportunities that advance both our financial and personal growth. We can take advantage of new opportunities, adjust to changing conditions, and move confidently and nimbly through the complexity of the financial landscape when we are always learning and developing.

The Meeting Point of Discipline and Mentality in Financial Independence: The key to achieving financial freedom lies at the nexus of discipline and mindset. Our financial goals are accelerated when we combine disciplined financial habits and behaviors with a mindset that is in accordance with wealth-building principles. This combination enables us to take advantage of our mindset's full potential, use discipline to make steady progress, and keep up our momentum while we pursue financial success. Furthermore, discipline and thinking go hand in hand in developing resilience, tenacity, and focus. While discipline gives the framework and consistency required to make dreams into reality, a positive mindset offers the drive and confidence in our capacity to reach financial freedom. Collectively, they serve as the cornerstone of an effective wealth-building plan that endures difficulties, adjusts to shifting circumstances, and maintains long-term financial stability.

Taking Initiative and Putting Plans into Practice

As we get to the end of our investigation into the concept that "Your wealth is your mindset," it is critical to stress the importance of putting plans into practice and acting upon them. Financial freedom can only be attained via proactive measures, dedication, and accountability. Consider the following crucial strategies:

Create Wealth-Creating a Mentality
Develop an attitude of abundance;

confront and refute money-related limiting beliefs; concentrate on impact and value creation; and adopt a growth-oriented viewpoint.

Develop Responsible Financial Habits: Establish and adhere to a budget; - Make regular and automated saves; Diversify your holdings and make prudent investments - Handle debt sensibly to prevent overspending

Make an Investment in Ongoing Education

Learn about investment, wealth management, and personal finance. Remain current on market developments, financial trends, and financial tactics. Seek advice from mentors or financial experts. Resilience and persistence are key. You should: - View setbacks as teaching opportunities - Continue to prioritize your long-term financial objectives Remain resilient in the face of economic hardships or market swings. Honor victories and advancements made along the way.

To sum up, "Your wealth is your mindset" captures the significant relationship that exists between discipline, mindset, and financial freedom. We can realize our potential for long-term wealth, security, and happiness by cultivating a good outlook, forming responsible financial habits, and making proactive efforts toward our financial objectives. Building wealth is only one step on the path to financial freedom; another is developing an attitude of abundance, resiliency, and constant improvement. Let's use discipline and a positive mindset to build a future of financial wealth, freedom, and fulfillment as we set out on our adventure.

CONCLUSION

The adage "Your wealth is your mindset" captures a fundamental reality that goes beyond simple financial plans and techniques in the context of personal finance and wealth creation. It addresses the fundamental ideas that guide our interactions with wealth, prosperity, and plenty. We have explored how discipline and mindset can lead to financial freedom, and we have looked closely at these ideas' transforming potential and how they affect our path to financial prosperity. The first step in achieving financial independence is taking care of ourselves mentally. Our mentality serves as a filter through which we view possibilities, negotiate obstacles, and make financial decisions. Having an abundance attitude instead of a scarcity mindset allows us to perceive wealth as an infinite resource that can be developed and shared, which opens up a world of opportunities. We can change our perspective from one of shortage and limitation to one of abundance and opportunity by practicing beliefs of abundance, thankfulness, and possibility.

Furthermore, the influence of attitude transcends material concerns and penetrates all facets of our existence. We can rise to difficulties, learn from our mistakes, and persevere in the face of difficulty when we have a growth mentality. It motivates us to keep looking for chances for development and progress and to regard failures as stepping stones to success. A positive outlook gives us resilience, drive, and a feeling of purpose that propels us toward our financial objectives with unyielding commitment.

While discipline offers the framework

and consistency required to translate goals into reality, mentality lays the groundwork for financial success. Discipline includes routines, attitudes, and acts that support our beliefs and long-term financial objectives. It entails making thoughtful decisions, choosing to put off immediate gratification in favor of delayed gratification, and sticking to our budgetary goals despite distractions and temptations.

Financial management involves many facets of discipline, such as debt management, investing, saving, and budgeting. Living within our means, avoiding needless costs, and prudently allocating money to our financial priorities are all vital. When it comes to investment techniques, discipline is even more important. Long-term thinking, research, and patience are all necessary for creating sustainable wealth.

Moreover, discipline goes beyond sound money management practices to include mindset discipline, or the capacity to control our feelings, ideas, and attitudes in a way that advances our financial objectives. It entails overcoming limiting beliefs, exercising self-control, and maintaining an optimistic outlook in the face of obstacles or failures from the outside world.

The combination of discipline and mindset is the real key to achieving financial freedom. A strong force that moves us closer to our financial goals is created when we combine a wealth-building attitude with disciplined financial behaviors and routines. Using the structure and consistency that discipline offers with the optimism, resiliency, and creativity of our mindset, this synergy enables us to fully utilize our mindset.

Decisions are made, habits are formed, and progress is maintained at the nexus of discipline and mentality. It gives us the confidence and clarity to negotiate the intricacies of the financial world, make wise financial decisions, and maintain our focus on long-term objectives. A strong sense of empowerment, ownership, and accountability for our financial well-being is fostered by the combination of discipline and mindset, which results in long-term financial plenty and freedom. Gaining financial independence by self-discipline and a growth mentality is an ongoing process that requires learning, adapting, and growing. It calls for us to create a growth mentality, which welcomes change, values criticism, and looks for chances to improve. Maintaining awareness of financial trends, investigating novel approaches, and modifying our habits and thinking to conform to new situations are all components of continuous progress. Furthermore, achieving financial freedom involves a path of personal growth and self-discovery. It calls on us to face our preconceived notions, anxieties, and restrictions around wealth, prosperity, and plenty. It asks us to reevaluate our conceptions of success and wealth in light of our beliefs and goals, as well as to question accepted knowledge and social standards.

It is crucial that we understand that obstacles and failures are a part of this journey and that they present priceless chances for development. Whether a financial decision is successful or not, it always teaches us something new and advances our understanding of how to create and manage money.

Although discipline and mentality are essential for financial success, the importance of support and community cannot be understated. Along the process, having mentors, advisors, and like-minded people around us who share our values, objectives, and vision can be a great source of accountability, support, and direction. Creating a network of experts, mentors, and peers that supports us allows us to take advantage of group knowledge, see things from other angles, and overcome obstacles more skillfully.

We can also improve our financial

confidence, abilities, and knowledge by getting professional counsel, going to seminars or workshops, and continuing our education. It is not intended for us to travel the path to financial independence alone, but rather in partnership with those who can push, encourage, and inspire us to achieve greater achievement.

In the midst of chasing financial independence, it's critical to take stock of our accomplishments and acknowledge the strides we've made. No matter how minor, celebrating our victories gives us the confidence boost we need to keep going forward, reinforce healthy behaviors, and keep moving forward. Every step you take toward financial freedom, whether it's saving enough money, investing wisely, or getting past a financial obstacle, should be celebrated.

To sum up, "Your wealth is your mindset" captures the idea that discipline and a positive outlook may lead to prosperity and financial freedom. We develop a roadmap for sustainable wealth creation and prosperity by combining a disciplined financial lifestyle with a positive mindset based on abundance, resilience, and growth. Building wealth is only one step in the process of achieving financial freedom; another is cultivating an attitude of empowerment, accountability, and ongoing improvement.

Let's embrace the power of discipline and mindset as drivers of success and change as we set out on our adventure. Let's make a commitment to developing a mindset of potential, abundance, and resilience while adhering to sound financial practices that support our objectives and core values. The foundation of a prosperous financial future, where plenty, security, and freedom are not just goals but actualized realities, is composed of mindset and discipline. Here's to achieving financial freedom with the application of discipline and a growth-oriented mindset; may your path be one of success and happiness.

www.ingramcontent.com/pod-product-compliance
Lightning Source LLC
Chambersburg PA
CBHW050304230526
45471CB00005B/2011